IF YOU WERE A...

Firefighter

IF YOU WERE A...
Firefighter

Virginia Schomp

BENCHMARK BOOKS

MARSHALL CAVENDISH
NEW YORK

If you were a firefighter, how high you could climb! Up you go to the top of the tallest ladder. Down below, it takes strong arms to carry the heavy hose that blasts water to put out the fire.

Will you go underwater? In your diver's suit, you keep cool battling a boatyard blaze. Will you try smoke jumping? Strap on your parachute. Jumping from airplanes gets you to forest fires fast!

Are you ready for the dangers and excitement you would face if you were a firefighter?

Bright flames and pitch-black smoke—the firefighter's world is red-hot and dangerous.

*Each firefighter has a special job to do . . .
and a special spot on the fire truck.*

*When the need is for speed,
stairs are too slow!*

Alarm bells sound in a city firehouse. "Turn out! Fire at Main and Third!" booms the loudspeaker.

In a flash, firefighters slide down the brass pole. They yank on their pants, boots, and coats. Within seconds, two fire trucks are racing down the street, sirens wailing and lights flashing.

6

Water from underground pipes rushes up through the fire hydrant, out the hoses, and onto the fire.

First to reach the fire is the pumper truck. Quickly the driver clamps a fat hose on a fire hydrant. Other firefighters stretch hoses from the pumper truck to the burning building. The truck's engine sucks water from the hydrant and shoots it out all the hoses fast and hard.

The men and women working the pumper's hoses are called the engine company. Each has a special job to do. If you were the nozzle person, you would aim a fountain of water at the flames. You would soak the building next door, too, to keep the fire from spreading.

Some people call the pumper truck the "fire engine," because its powerful engine pumps water to put out fires.

Ladder trucks—sometimes called "hook-and-ladders"—are packed with ladders, hooks, axes, and other cutting tools.

Here comes the tiller person, perched in a cab high atop the rear of the ladder truck.

Up speeds the ladder company in the ladder truck. This long truck carries lots of firefighting and rescue equipment. To turn corners, it must bend in two. The chauffeur *(show-FER)* steers the front wheels. The tiller person steers the back.

Some aerial ladders reach higher than 100 feet. That's taller than a ten-story building!

Firefighters risk their own lives to save people trapped in burning buildings.

The ladder company's most important job is rescuing people from the burning building. The tall aerial ladder shoots up like a jack-in-the-box. Firefighters crawl through a window. Bending below the smoke, they search for anyone who needs help. Air masks and air tanks help them breathe. Helmets protect their heads from falling wood and bricks.

Axes smash, saws whine, hooks rip metal. The ladder company breaks holes in the roof and windows. The holes let out hot air and smoke. Now the engine company firefighters can drag in their hoses.

The nozzle person twists the hose tip. With a hiss, cool wet fog fills the room.

Breaking holes in this apartment house will make it safer and easier to fight the fire.

Five-alarm fire! The fire chief calls for five fire companies to battle a big blaze.

The fire chief helps all the firefighters work together as a team. The chief barks orders into a two-way radio—"Search the basement! Bring more hoses!"

If the fire gets too big, the chief calls for help. Companies from other fire departments join the action. Special trucks bring extra firefighting equipment and first-aid supplies to help injured people.

Wrestling heavy hoses, chopping through doors and rooftops—fighting fires is exhausting work.

At last the fire is beaten. The tired, dirty firefighters stamp out every last spark. Then they roll up their hoses and head back to their firehouse.

The firehouse is like a second home to city fire-fighters. They take turns living and sleeping there. They clean and test their equipment there. Like a family, they share cooking and housecleaning chores and enjoy relaxing together.

A fire crew relaxes but stays ready to roll the minute the next alarm sounds.

Country and small-town firefighters do not live at their firehouse. They are volunteers, not paid workers like city firefighters. Most of the time, volunteers work at other jobs. They may be bankers or farmers, teachers or students.

In farm country, volunteers hurry from their homes or jobs to fight fires.

No fire hydrant? No problem! This tanker-pumper pours a poolful from its giant tank.

If you were a volunteer firefighter, you might keep a special radio in your pocket. Suddenly it beeps and crackles—"Fire on Mill Road!" You drop everything, hop in your car, and hurry to catch up with the pumper truck.

There are few fire hydrants in the countryside, so pumpers carry their own water. When that runs out, the volunteers dip a hose in a well, pond, or portable water tank. The pumper sucks up the water like soda through a straw.

Divers, rescue workers, and other brave firefighters search for people trapped by rising floodwaters.

Firefighters must be ready for any emergency. The fire department helps people hurt in accidents or caught in floods.

In waterfront areas, firefighters battle fires on ships and docks. Their fireboat sucks all the water it needs from the river or bay.

Sometimes the fire is too hot. The fireboat cannot get close. Then specially trained firefighters put on diver's suits and air tanks. In the cool water, they can swim right up to the hottest blaze.

Some fireboats can spray as much water as ten pumper trucks!

Firefighters in wooded areas may use shovels to fight forest fires. Digging through the leaves and grass, they clear a strip of bare dirt. When the fire roars up to this fire line, it stops dead. There's nothing left to burn.

A fire has started in the woods, far from any roads. Fly in the smoke jumpers! These firefighters parachute down from planes or helicopters. Smoke jumpers always carry rope. It comes in handy if you get stuck in a treetop.

Help comes from the sky as a helicopter bombs the woods with water.

Dirt shoveled over crackling flames helps to tame this forest fire.

In the woods and on the water, in small towns and big cities, wherever and whenever they are needed, firefighters come running. Their work is hard and dangerous. It is full of action. Would you like to be a firefighter?

You can start by learning how to prevent fires and what to do in case there is a fire. When you are older, you may go to fire training school. There you will learn how to fight fires and save lives.

Can you imagine how proud you would feel if you were a firefighter?

Even getting dressed takes practice when your clothes and gear weigh up to 100 pounds.

At fire training school, students learn to trust their fire belts to prevent falls.

FIREFIGHTING IN TIME

Early Americans fought fires by passing buckets of water from hand to hand along a line of people called a bucket brigade.

The first fire engines were called hand pumpers. It took a team of strong men to pull these heavy machines to a fire and press the pump handles.

Later, horses pulled the wagons and steam engines worked the pumps.

In the early 1900s, gasoline-powered fire trucks replaced the fire horses. Fire dogs lost their jobs, too. Once every firehouse had a dalmatian to keep other dogs away from the galloping horses. Today dalmatians are the firefighters' mascot and friend.

Women have been volunteer firefighters since America's earliest days. They first became paid firefighters in 1974.

A FIREFIGHTER'S CLOTHING AND TOOLS

Helmets, coats, and boots—made of special material for protection from heat and flames

Fire ax and pick—for breaking open doors, walls, windows, and roofs

Heavy gloves— to protect hands

Air masks and air tanks—worn in smoke-filled places; pike poles— for smashing windows

Fire extinguisher—for putting out small fires

Power saw—for cutting through metal or thick wood

WORDS TO KNOW

aerial ladder   A very long ladder attached to a fire truck. A motor raises, lowers, and moves the ladder.

chauffeur (show-FER)   The firefighter who drives the front wheels of a ladder truck.

engine company   The crew of the pumper truck. The engine company's main job is to put out fires.

fire line   Ground near a forest fire that has been cleared of trees, leaves, and anything else that might burn.

ladder company   The crew of the ladder truck. The ladder company's main jobs are to rescue people from burning buildings and to break holes to let out heat and smoke.

nozzle person   The firefighter who aims the hose at a fire.

smoke jumpers   Firefighters who parachute jump from airplanes or helicopters to fight forest fires.

tiller person   The firefighter who drives the rear wheels of a ladder truck.

This book is for Christopher, funny and fearless nephew

Benchmark Books
Marshall Cavendish Corporation
99 White Plains Road
Tarrytown, New York 10591
Copyright© 1998 by Marshall Cavendish Corporation

Library of Congress Cataloging-in-Publication Data
Schomp, Virginia   If You Were A Firefighter / Virginia Schomp.
p.   cm. — (If you were a—)   Includes bibliographical references and index.
Summary: Explains what firefighters do and what equipment they use to put out fires.
!SBN 0-7614-0615-8
1. Fire extinction—Juvenile literature. 2. Fire fighters—Juvenile literature. [1. Fire fighters. 2. Fire extinction. 3. Occupations.]
I. Title. II. Series   TH914.S36   1998   363.37'092—DC20   96-35142   CIP   AC

Photo research by Debbie Needleman

Front cover: *Thomas Wanstall/The Image Works*
Back cover: *Robert Maass*

The photographs in this book are used by permission and through the courtesy of: *Harvey Eisner*: title page, 14-15, 23 (left), 30 (bottom center), 30 (bottom left). *Henry Horenstein*: 2, 8 (left). *Arms Communications*: Douglas Zalud, 4-5; Hans Halberstadt, 29 (top). *Uniphoto Picture Agency*: Carl Purcell, 6; Bob Llewellyn, 16 (inset). *Robert Maass*: 6-7, 10, 18, 30 (top right), 30 (center). *The Image Works*: Frozen Images, 8 (right); Thomas Wanstall, 16-17, 26; Bob Daemmrich, 27. *Keith D. Cullom*: 9, 13, 21, 22, 30 (bottom right). *Bill Noonan*: 11. *The Picture Cube*: C. Blankenhorn, 12; Robert Finken, 29 (bottom); Aneal Vohra, 31. *The Image Bank*: Flip Chalfant, 19; Grant Faint, 30 (top left). *AP/The Press Democrat, Annie Wells*: 23 (right). *Laurance B. Aiuppy*: 24. *Nita Winter*: 25. *CIGNA Museum & Art Collection*: 28 (top left). *The Granger Collection, New York*: 28 (top right), 28 (bottom).

Printed in the United States of America
3   5   7   8   6   4   2

INDEX